"***Tia Cooper*** has crafted a bold and needed guide for every believer who is ready to rise from survival mode into their Spirit-filled identity. *If You Can Be Anything, B/YOU* is more than a devotional; it is a 90-day awakening that calls you to reclaim who God created you to be and walk in that truth with courage. I gladly endorse this transformative work that strengthens hearts, clarifies purpose, and releases FREEdom in its readers."

Rev. Dr. Major A. Stewart, Senior Pastor
Greater Mt. Sinai Baptist Church, Charlotte, NC,
Author of Mind Over Storms

"***Tia Cooper*** has given the body of Christ a timely gift. *If You Can Be Anything, B/YOU* is a 90-day journey that leads you out of insecurity and into your God-given identity. With Scripture, honest reflection, and powerful declarations, Tia shows that you are chosen, known, loved, and created in the image of God. This devotional doesn't just inspire; it coaches you to live boldly and authentically before the Lord. I wholeheartedly endorse Tia Cooper and this work, believing many lives will be strengthened and set free through these pages."

Pastor David Hawkins
Senior Pastor of Living The Word Church
Author of *Dips Disruptions, and Destiny*
MDIV, MBA

"This devotional is a timely and gentle reminder of who God says we are. Each day confidently guides readers back to their identity in Christ. It is scripture-centered, soul-healing, and deeply affirming. Everyone will benefit from this book in their quiet time."

Tiffany Jones

IF YOU CAN BE ANYTHING... B/YOU

TIA COOPER

Names: Cooper, Tia.

Title: If/ Tia Cooper.

Summary: "If You Can Be Anything, B/YOU is a powerful 90-day devotional that helps you drop the masks, break free from false labels, and walk boldly in your God-given identity with breakthrough and freedom."— Provided by the author.

Identifiers: ISBN 978-1-954624-34-4 (paperback)

ISBN 978-1-954624-35-1 (ebook)

Library of Congress Control Number: 2026931738

Subjects: BISAC: RELIGION / Christian Living / Devotional (REL012020)
RELIGION / Christian Living / Personal Growth (REL012070)
RELIGION / Christian Living / Spiritual Growth (REL012120)

Published by JT Publishing, Spartanburg, South Carolina
www.jtpublishinghouse.com

Printed in the United States of America

10 9 8 7 6 5 4 3 2 1

DEDICATION

This book is dedicated to everyone who has struggled to understand their identity and worth.

If you have ever worn a mask to fit in, doubted your value, or questioned if you belong—this devotional was written for you.

You are not forgotten. Your identity is not defined by others' opinions, your past, or inner doubts. You are defined by the One who made you, calls you by name, and declares you chosen, loved, and enough.

May these words remind you that your identity is already secure in Christ, not something you must earn.

If you can be anything, B/YOU.

HOW TO USE THIS 90-DAY DEVOTIONAL

Welcome to your 90-day journey of becoming who God already says you are. This devotional is designed to be more than something you read—it's something you practice. Each day follows a simple rhythm to help you build spiritual consistency, renew your mind, and walk in freedom.

Start with the Scripture. Read it slowly, then read it again. Ask the Holy Spirit to highlight one phrase for you to carry throughout the day. Don't rush—let the Word do what it was sent to do.

Sit with the Devotional Thought. Use it as a mirror, not a measuring stick. This isn't about perfection; it's about alignment. Let truth confront the labels, lies, and masks that no longer fit your identity in Christ.

Pray it out loud. These prayers are written to help you respond to God, not perform for Him. If a line doesn't match your current season, personalize it— make it honest and make it yours.

Answer the Reflection. Write your response if you can (even a few sentences). Transformation happens when truth becomes personal. If you're doing this with a group, use the reflection as your discussion starter.

Speak the Declaration with faith. Your words matter. Declarations train your heart to agree with heaven—especially on days your emotions try to argue. Say it anyway. Believe it again.

Finally, don't aim to "finish" this devotional—aim to be formed by it. Take your time, repeat days when needed, and let these 90 days mark a new beginning: boldness, breakthrough, and freedom—B/YOU, in Christ.

TABLE OF CONTENTS

DAY 1
CHOSEN BUT NOT FORGOTTEN

Scripture: "But you are a chosen generation, a royal priesthood, a holy nation, His own special people…" —*1 Peter 2:9 (NKJV)*

Devotional Thought: You are not random or forgotten. Before anyone else knew your name, God declared you chosen. He didn't just save you—He selected you. You belong to a kingdom that cannot be shaken, and your identity is secure in Christ. Walk in the confidence of knowing that you are set apart for something divine. The plans that He has for you go beyond what you could imagine. How could God, who made you, forget you?

Prayer: Lord, thank You for choosing me before anyone else ever knew my name. Help me to live boldly as someone handpicked by You. Let me not chase after the approval of others, but rest in the truth that I belong to You. Remind me each day that I am set apart for a divine purpose. In Jesus' name, Amen.

Reflection: What would change in my life if I genuinely believed God chose me?

Declaration: If you can be anything, B/YOU.

DAY 2
KNOWN AND LOVED

Scripture: "Before I formed you in the womb I knew you, and before you were born I consecrated you…" —*Jeremiah 1:5 (ESV)*

Devotional Thought: God didn't stumble upon you—He formed you. Your identity was born in His heart long before the world saw it. You are not trying to earn love; you are created from God's love. He knows every part of you and still chooses you. That's not rejection—that's redemption.

Prayer: Father, I praise You that You fully know me. You see my heart, my struggles, and my victories, and still love me. Teach me to walk openly before You and receive Your unconditional love. Help me let go of fear and shame, knowing that I am secure in You. In Jesus' name, Amen.

Reflection: Where have I been hiding from God's love instead of receiving it?

Declaration: If you can be anything, B/YOU.

DAY 3
IMAGE BEARER

Scripture: "So God created man in His own image, in the image of God He created him; male and female He created them." —*Genesis 1:27 (NKJV)*

Devotional Thought: You are crafted in the image of God, not just to reflect His beauty, but to reflect His nature. You carry His creativity, His authority, and His compassion. When you look in the mirror, see more than flaws—see the fingerprint of the Divine.

Prayer: Creator God, thank You for designing me in Your image. Let my life reflect Your

compassion, creativity, and love to those around
me. Give me the courage to see myself through
Your eyes, not through the lens of insecurity.
Help me carry Your likeness with honor each
day. In Jesus' name, Amen.

Reflection: Do I see myself as someone made
in the image of God? Why or why not?

Declaration: If you can be anything, B/YOU.

DAY 4
GOD'S MASTERPIECE

Scripture: "For we are God's masterpiece. He has created us anew in Christ Jesus, so we can do the good things He planned for us long ago." —*Ephesians 2:10 (NLT)*

Devotional Thought: You're not a mistake in progress—you are God's masterpiece. That means He's intentional about every detail of your life. God created you with purpose and for purpose. Let go of the pressure to be perfect. Just be positioned in Him.

Prayer: God, thank You for creating me on purpose and with purpose. When I doubt myself, remind me that I am Your masterpiece—carefully designed and deeply valued. Help me rest in who You made me to be and walk confidently in what You've already planned for my life. In Jesus' name, Amen.

Reflection: What "imperfections" have I let define me? How does seeing myself as God's masterpiece shift my mindset?

Declaration: If you can be anything, B/YOU.

DAY 5
SECURE IN CHRIST

Scripture: "Therefore, if anyone is in Christ, he is a new creation. The old has passed away; behold, the new has come."—*2 Corinthians 5:17 (ESV)*

Devotional Thought: You are not who you were. When you said "yes" to Christ, your identity changed. You don't have to wear the shame of your past because Christ clothed you in righteousness. You are secure, stable, and sustained by the One who calls you new.

Prayer: Father, thank You that I am a new creation in Christ. Break every chain of my past and remind me of the freedom I have in

You. Please give me the strength to walk away from shame and step into victory. Let my life be evidence of Your transforming power. In Jesus' name, Amen.

Reflection: Am I living from my new identity, or am I still chained to my old one?

Declaration: If you can be anything, B/YOU.

DAY 6
CALLED FOR MORE

Scripture: "You didn't choose me. I chose you. I appointed you to go and produce lasting fruit…"—*John 15:16 (NLT)*

Devotional Thought: God called you for more than survival—He called you for fruitfulness. You and everything about you are designed to produce, not perform. You weren't just saved; you were sent. The fruit of your identity isn't in how loud you shout—it's in how deeply you're rooted.

Prayer: Lord, thank You for choosing and appointing me for fruit that lasts. Keep me rooted in You so my life produces purpose, not performance. Help me live sent, secure, and fruitful in You. In Jesus' name, Amen.

Reflection: What fruit is my life producing? What in my life needs pruning so more can grow?

Declaration: If you can be anything, B/YOU.

DAY 7
AUTHENTICALLY YOU

Scripture: "...who gave Himself for us, that He might redeem us from every lawless deed and purify for Himself *His* own special people, zealous for good works."—*Titus 2:14 (NKJV)*

Devotional Thought: Your identity in Christ isn't a mask—it's a mirror. You don't need to dim your light to fit in. God made you uniquely, intentionally, and boldly. Authenticity isn't rebellion; it's revelation. When you show up as your authentic self in Christ, you give others permission to do the same.

Prayer: Father, thank You for creating me with purpose and light. Give me the courage to live authentically in You, never hiding what You placed inside me. Let my life reflect Your goodness and bring glory back to You. In Jesus' name, Amen.

Reflection: What parts of my authentic self am I hiding? Why am I hiding those things?

Declaration: If you can be anything, B/YOU.

WEEK 1
PRAYER FOCUS

Father, thank You for the truths revealed this week. Help me to live them out daily, walk in Your strength, and stand firm in my identity in Christ. Let my life bring glory to You. In Jesus' name, Amen.

WEEKLY THOUGHTS

DAY 8
FREE INDEED
(PART I)

Scripture: "So if the Son sets you free, you will be free indeed."—*John 8:36 (ESV)*

Devotional Thought: Freedom is not a feeling—it's a fact secured in Christ. When Jesus set you free, He didn't just unlock the door; He tore down the prison. You are not held captive by your past, your fears, or your failures. Live like someone who's already free, not like someone still trying to escape.

Prayer: Jesus, I celebrate the freedom You gave me through the cross. Help me never to return to the things that once held me captive. Teach me to live with joy as one who has been set free. May my freedom point others back to You. In Jesus' name, Amen.

Reflection: Am I walking in the freedom Christ already gave me, or am I still holding onto chains He broke?

Declaration: If you can be anything, B/YOU.

DAY 9
REDEEMED

Scripture: "Let the redeemed of the Lord say so, whom He has redeemed from the hand of the enemy."—*Psalm 107:2 (NKJV)*

Devotional Thought: To be redeemed means you've been bought back, repurchased by God. God didn't just find you—He fought for you. He saw your brokenness and still said, "You're worth it." Your restoration isn't based on what you lost, but on who you've become in Him. Speak like someone who is redeemed.

Prayer: Lord, thank You for redeeming me and restoring my brokenness. Help me remember that my worth is secured in You, not in my past. Let my story be a testimony of Your grace. Keep me walking in the fullness of Your restoration. In Jesus' name, Amen.

Reflection: In what area of my life do I need to embrace restoration?

Declaration: If you can be anything, B/YOU.

DAY 10
ROOTED IN GRACE

Scripture: "Let your roots grow down into Him, and let your lives be built on Him."—*Colossians 2:7 (NLT)*

Devotional Thought: Your identity will only flourish when your roots go deep into grace. The world says to build on success, status, or image. But God says, "Build on Me." When your life is rooted in Christ, storms may come—but you won't be shaken.

Prayer: Lord, I thank You for the gift of grace that strengthens me daily. When I feel weak, remind me that Your power is made perfect in my weakness. Keep me anchored in Your love and steady in my walk. Help me to rely entirely on Your strength. In Jesus' name, Amen.

Reflection: What have I been building my identity on? Is it helping me grow, or is it making me feel empty?

Declaration: If you can be anything, B/YOU.

DAY 11
FEARFULLY AND WONDERFULLY MADE (PART I)

Scripture: "I praise you because I am fearfully and wonderfully made; your works are wonderful; I know that full well."—*Psalm 139:14 (NIV)*

Devotional Thought: You are not ordinary. You are wonderfully made—designed by God's own hands. Every part of you carries His intentionality. Stop comparing yourself to others. You are not a copy—you are a creation. And God doesn't make mistakes.

Prayer: Lord, I thank You for making me fearfully and wonderfully. Remove every doubt and comparison that tries to steal my confidence. Teach me to celebrate the unique way You created me, body, mind, and spirit. May I live each day in gratitude for being a living reflection of Your intentional design. In Jesus' name, Amen.

Reflection: What lies have I believed about my worth? I will replace the lies today with this truth: "I am wonderfully made."

Declaration: If you can be anything, B/YOU.

DAY 12

ADOPTED AND ACCEPTED (PART I)

Scripture: "God decided in advance to adopt us into His own family by bringing us to Himself through Jesus Christ."—*Ephesians 1:5 (NLT)*

Devotional Thought: You are not an outsider trying to earn a place—God adopted you into His family. You don't have to perform to belong. Christ fully accepts you. Your identity is not in who rejected you, but in who received you.

Prayer: Father, I praise You for adopting me into Your family through Christ. Please help me live as one who is already accepted, not striving for approval from others. Remind me that rejection has no power over me because I belong to You. Let my heart rest in the security of Your unconditional love. In Jesus' name, Amen.

Reflection: Am I living like a child of God or like an orphan still searching for acceptance?

Declaration: If you can be anything, B/YOU.

DAY 13
BOLD AND COURAGEOUS

Scripture: "Be strong and courageous. Do not be afraid… for the Lord your God goes with you."—*Deuteronomy 31:6 (NIV)*

Devotional Thought: God doesn't call the qualified—He qualifies the called. Your identity in Him gives you access to boldness and courage, not because of your strength but because of His presence. Courage is not the absence of fear—it's moving forward despite it.

Prayer: Lord, I thank You for the courage that comes from knowing You are with me. Strengthen me to face every challenge with faith instead of fear. Please help me to take bold steps in obedience, even when the path feels uncertain. Let my life be a testimony of Your presence and power at work in me. In Jesus' name, Amen.

Reflection: Where in my life do I need to rise in boldness today?

Declaration: If you can be anything, B/YOU.

DAY 14
ANOINTED FOR THIS

Scripture: "But you have an anointing from the Holy One, and you know all things."—*1 John 2:20 (NKJV)*

Devotional Thought: You are equipped and anointed. God has placed a divine enablement on your life to do what He created you to do. The anointing breaks yokes, brings clarity, and empowers purpose. Stop shrinking. You are anointed for this.

Prayer: Lord, I thank You for anointing me with Your Spirit for the assignment on my life. Remind me that it is not by my strength but by

Your power that I can accomplish what You've called me to do. Remove fear, doubt, and hesitation, and replace them with bold faith. Let me walk confidently, knowing I am equipped and empowered for this very moment. In Jesus' name, Amen.

Reflection: What would shift in my life if I truly believed God anointed me?

Declaration: If you can be anything, B/YOU

WEEK 2
PRAYER FOCUS

Father, thank You for the truths revealed this week. Help me to live them out daily, walk in Your strength, and stand firm in my identity in Christ. Let my life bring glory to You. In Jesus' name, Amen.

WEEKLY THOUGHTS

DAY 15
SEATED WITH CHRIST (PART I)

Scripture: "And God raised us up with Christ and seated us with Him in the heavenly realms in Christ Jesus."—*Ephesians 2:6 (NIV)*

Devotional Thought: You are not beneath— you are seated with Christ. That's a position of power, not pressure. You don't fight for victory; you fight from victory. Your identity grants you spiritual authority. Don't settle for the floor when God placed you at the table.

Prayer: Father, Thank You for raising me up and seating me with Christ. Help me live from victory, not striving, and walk in the authority You've given me through Him. Teach me to see myself from heaven's perspective and move with confidence in who I am in Christ. In Jesus' name, Amen.

Reflection: Am I living like someone seated in heavenly places—or like someone stuck on the sidelines?

Declaration: If you can be anything, B/YOU.

DAY 16
LIGHT IN THE DARKNESS

Scripture: "You are the light of the world. A city set on a hill cannot be hidden."—*Matthew 5:14 (ESV)*

Devotional Thought: You aren't made to blend in—you are made to stand out. You aren't made to blend in—you are made to stand out. Your identity in Christ makes you a beacon of hope, not a shadow in the background. Shine unapologetically. The world doesn't need perfection. It needs light. And you carry it.

Prayer: Father, thank You for making me the light of the world. Shine through me in every space I enter, even in dark places. Give me the courage to stand boldly as a reflection of Your truth. Let my light lead others closer to You. In Jesus' name, Amen.

Reflection: Where have I been dimming my light out of fear, insecurity, or shame?

Declaration: If you can be anything, B/YOU.

DAY 17
HOLY AND SET APART

Scripture: "But now, thus says the Lord, who created you…'Fear not, for I have redeemed you; I have called you by your name; you are Mine.'"—*Isaiah 43:1 (NKJV)*

Devotional Thought: God didn't call you to be average—He called you to be set apart. You are not common. Your identity is wrapped in holiness, not hype. He knows your name and has marked you for Himself. Don't apologize for being different. You're designed that way.

Reflection: Am I compromising my uniqueness to fit into a space God never called me to?

Prayer: Father, I thank You for calling me by name and setting me apart for Your glory. Help me to embrace holiness, not as a burden, but as the honor of belonging fully to You. Strengthen me to resist the pull of conformity and to walk in purity of heart and purpose. Let my life shine as evidence of Your sanctifying power. In Jesus' name, Amen.

Declaration: If you can be anything, B/YOU.

DAY 18
PROTECTED BY PURPOSE

Scripture: "The Lord will fulfill His purpose for me; your steadfast love, O Lord, endures forever."—*Psalm 138:8 (ESV)*

Devotional Thought: Angels do not just protect you—you are protected by purpose. There are things that could not and cannot touch you because of what God planned through you. Your identity comes with divine coverage. When you understand that, fear loses its grip.

Prayer: Lord, I praise You for the covering that comes with Your purpose for my life. Thank You that no weapon formed against me can prosper, because You are directing my steps. Teach me to walk with courage, knowing that destiny shields me from destruction. Keep me confident in the safety of Your plan. In Jesus' name, Amen.

Reflection: What threats or lies am I giving power to that my purpose already defeated?

Declaration: If you can be anything, B/YOU.

DAY 19
VICTORIOUS IN CHRIST

Scripture: "But thanks be to God! He gives us the victory through our Lord Jesus Christ." —*1 Corinthians 15:57 (NIV)*

Devotional Thought: You're not fighting for a win—you're living from a win. In Christ, you are not a victim of your circumstances. You are victorious over them. The cross settled it. The resurrection sealed it. And your faith activates it.

Prayer: Lord, I thank You for the victory that is already mine through Jesus Christ. Please help me to live each day with the confidence that I am not fighting for victory but from victory. Remind me that no circumstance, setback, or struggle can overcome the power of the cross. Let my life reflect the triumph of Your resurrection in all that I do. In Jesus' name, Amen.

Reflection: What areas of my life need to shift to a victorious mindset?

Declaration: If you can be anything, B/YOU.

DAY 20
HIDDEN IN CHRIST

Scripture: "He who dwells in the secret place of the Most High shall abide under the shadow of the Almighty."—*Psalm 91:1 (NIV)*

Devotional Thought: The real you isn't in your resume, your reputation, or your reflection—it's hidden in Christ. That means the world doesn't get to define you. God does. Your identity is protected, preserved, and placed in a position no one can strip from you.

Prayer: Father, I thank You that my actual life is hidden with Christ in You. Teach me to rest in the safety of Your covering rather than seeking validation from the world. Protect me from distractions that try to pull me away from my identity in You. May I live with peace, knowing that who I truly am is secure in Your hands. In Jesus' name, Amen.

Reflection: Am I searching for my identity in people or resting in who God says I am?

Declaration: If you can be anything, B/YOU.

DAY 21
STRENGTHENED BY GRACE

Scripture: "Be strong in the grace that is in Christ Jesus."—*2 Timothy 2:1 (NKJV)*

Devotional Thought: Grace is not just a covering—it's a strength. You don't have to be everything when you're in the One who is. Your identity is powered by grace, not striving. When you feel weak, grace says, "You're still enough." When you fall, grace says, "You're still Mine."

Prayer: Lord, I thank You for the gift of grace that strengthens me daily. When I feel weak, remind me that Your power is made perfect in my weakness. Keep me anchored in Your love and steady in my walk. Help me to rely entirely on Your strength. In Jesus' name, Amen.

Reflection: Where do I need to stop striving and start standing in grace?

Declaration: If you can be anything, B/YOU.

WEEK 3
PRAYER FOCUS

Father, thank You for the truths revealed this week. Help me to live them out daily, walk in Your strength, and stand firm in my identity in Christ. Let my life bring glory to You. In Jesus' name, Amen.

WEEKLY THOUGHTS

DAY 22
CONFIDENT IN CHRIST

Scripture: "So do not throw away your confidence; it will be richly rewarded."—*Hebrews 10:35 (NIV)*

Devotional Thought: Confidence doesn't come from what you've done—it comes from who you are in Christ. Don't trade your God-given confidence for people-pleasing or self-doubt. You are fully known, fully loved, and fully equipped. Walk boldly. The reward is already promised.

Prayer: Father, I'm grateful for the confidence You've placed within me through Christ. Help me to guard it, walk boldly in it, and never trade it for fear or approval. Strengthen me to live fully assured of who I am in You. In Jesus' name, Amen.

Reflection: What have I let rob me of my God-given confidence?

Declaration: If you can be anything, B/YOU.

DAY 23
A NEW NAME

Scripture: "I will give them a white stone with a new name written on it, known only to the one who receives it."—*Revelation 2:17 (NIV)*

Devotional Thought: You are not who you used to be. When God saves you, He renames you. He replaces labels like "rejected," "broken," or "unworthy" with words like "beloved," "healed," and "chosen." Your new name is your new identity—and no one can take it away.

Prayer: Lord, I thank You for giving me a new name and a new identity in Christ. Please help me to release every label of shame, fear, or rejection that once defined me. Teach me to walk boldly in the truth of who You say I am. Let my words and actions reflect the transformation that comes only from You. In Jesus' name, Amen.

Reflection: What name or label do I need to let go of so I can live in my true identity?

Declaration: If you can be anything, B/YOU.

DAY 24
A FRIEND OF GOD (PART I)

Scripture: "I no longer call you servants… Instead, I have called you friends…"—*John 15:15 (NIV)*

Devotional Thought: You're not just a follower—you're a friend. God doesn't just want your obedience; He desires intimacy. Your identity includes a seat close to His heart, where you're not only known but confided in. There is no greater honor than being called His friend.

Prayer: Father, I thank You for the privilege of being called Your friend. Teach me to walk in closeness with You, sharing my heart in prayer and listening for Yours in return. Remove anything that hinders intimacy, and let me value Your presence above all else. May my life reflect the joy of true friendship with You. In Jesus' name, Amen.

Reflection: How does knowing God calls me His friend change how I relate to Him?

Declaration: If you can be anything, B/YOU.

DAY 25
EMPOWERED BY THE SPIRIT (PART I)

Scripture: "But you will receive power when the Holy Spirit comes on you…"—*Acts 1:8 (NIV)*

Devotional Thought: You are not powerless. You have the Holy Spirit living inside you, empowering you to do what you couldn't do on your own. Your identity includes divine ability—not to boast, but to be bold. You are not meant to do life by yourself.

Prayer: Holy Spirit, I thank You for filling me with Your power and presence. Remind me daily that it is not by might nor by strength, but by Your Spirit that I can overcome and accomplish all things. Stir up every gift You've placed within me and give me boldness to use them for Your glory. Let my life demonstrate the power of Your Spirit at work in me. In Jesus' name, Amen.

Reflection: Am I relying on my own strength or the Spirit's power in this season?

Declaration: If you can be anything, B/YOU.

DAY 26
COVERED
AND CLOTHED

Scripture: "I will greatly rejoice in the Lord… for He has clothed me with the garments of salvation, He has covered me with the robe of righteousness."—*Isaiah 61:10 (NKJV)*

Devotional Thought: You are not exposed—you are covered. God didn't just cleanse you; He clothed you. Your past is no longer your outfit. You are robed in righteousness, wrapped in grace, and crowned with love. Dress in your identity, not in your insecurity.

Prayer: Lord, I thank You that I am covered by Your blood and clothed in righteousness. Remind me that shame and guilt have no hold on me because I am wrapped in Your grace. Teach me to walk with confidence, knowing I wear the garments of salvation You freely provided. Let my life reflect the dignity and honor of being clothed in Christ. In Jesus' name, Amen.

Reflection: Am I still wearing the garments of guilt, or have I embraced His covering?

Declaration: If you can be anything, B/YOU.

DAY 27
SALT OF THE EARTH (PART I)

Scripture: "You are the salt of the earth…" —*Matthew 5:13 (NIV)*

Devotional Thought: Salt adds flavor and preserves what matters. That's your role in the world—not to fade in, but to make a difference. Your identity adds value to every space you enter. You are here to preserve truth, spark change, and make God's goodness undeniable.

Prayer: Father, I thank You for calling me to be the salt of the earth. Please help me bring flavor, preservation, and healing everywhere I go. Keep my words seasoned with grace and my actions filled with love that reflects You. Let my life make others thirst for Your presence. In Jesus' name, Amen.

Reflection: Where has God called me to bring flavor and preserve His truth?

Declaration: If you can be anything, B/YOU.

DAY 28
NO CONDEMNATION

Scripture: "Therefore, there is now no condemnation for those who are in Christ Jesus."—*Romans 8:1 (NIV)*

Devotional Thought: Shame is not your portion. Condemnation has no home in your identity. Guilt is exchanged for grace, and punishment is replaced with peace in Christ. You are not disqualified—you are delivered. Let go of the voice of the accuser and listen to the voice of your Redeemer.

Prayer: Lord, I thank You that there is now no condemnation for those who are in Christ

Jesus. Free my heart from the weight of guilt and shame that the enemy tries to place on me. Teach me to walk in the confidence of Your forgiveness and the freedom of Your grace. Help me to live unashamed, knowing I am covered by Your mercy. In Jesus' name, Amen.

Reflection: Am I letting the enemy condemn me for what God has already forgiven?

Declaration: If you can be anything, B/YOU.

WEEK 4
PRAYER FOCUS

Father, thank You for the truths revealed this week. Help me to live them out daily, walk in Your strength, and stand firm in my identity in Christ. Let my life bring glory to You. In Jesus' name, Amen.

WEEKLY THOUGHTS

DAY 29
CREATED FOR GOOD WORKS

Scripture: "In the same way, let your light shine before others, that they may see your good deeds and glorify your Father in heaven." —*Matthew 5:16 (NIV)*

Devotional Thought: You were never an accident—you are God's masterpiece. Designed with purpose, intention, and creativity. Your identity is not just about being—it's about doing. God created you with good works in mind that no one else can do like you.

Prayer: Father, I thank You that I was created in Christ Jesus for good works that You prepared in advance for me to do. Remind me daily that my life has purpose beyond what I see. Give me wisdom to recognize opportunities to serve and courage to step into them. Let my works bring glory to You and reflect the love of Christ to others. In Jesus' name, Amen.

Reflection: Am I walking in the works God prepared for me or shrinking back from them?

Declaration: If you can be anything, B/YOU.

DAY 30
JOY IS PART OF YOU

Scripture: "The joy of the Lord is your strength." —*Nehemiah 8:10 (NIV)*

Devotional Thought: Joy is not just a feeling— it's part of your identity. The world offers happiness that fades, but God provides joy that sustains. Even in hard seasons, joy can overflow because your strength doesn't come from circumstances; it comes from the Lord.

Prayer: Lord, I thank You that true joy is found in Your presence and is a permanent part of who I am in Christ. Remind me that joy is not based on circumstances but on the unshakable foundation of Your love. Teach me to carry joy as a testimony to others, even in difficult seasons. Let my life overflow with gladness that points people back to You. In Jesus' name, Amen.

Reflection: Where do I need to reclaim joy as my strength?

Declaration: If you can be anything, B/YOU.

DAY 31
CHOSEN, NOT CHASING

Scripture: "You did not choose me, but I chose you and appointed you…"—*John 15:16 (NIV)*

Devotional Thought: Stop chasing validation—God already chose you. God picked you on purpose. You don't have to audition for a role He already gave you. You're not chasing a seat—you've been assigned one.

Prayer: Lord, thank You for choosing me before anyone else ever knew my name. Help me to live boldly as someone handpicked by You.

Let me not chase after the approval of others but rest in the truth that I belong to You. Remind me each day that I am set apart for divine purpose. In Jesus' name, Amen.

Reflection: Where in my life am I trying to earn what God has already freely given me?

Declaration: If you can be anything, B/YOU.

DAY 32
SECURE IN HIS LOVE

Scripture: "Nothing will be able to separate us from the love of God that is in Christ Jesus our Lord."—*Romans 8:39 (NIV)*

Devotional Thought: There's nothing you can do to lose God's love. That's security. His love isn't based on your performance—it's rooted in His promise. You don't have to earn it, prove it, or fear losing it. In Christ, your identity is eternally secure.

Prayer: Father, I thank You that nothing can separate me from Your love. When doubts or fears try to shake me, remind me that I am held securely in Your arms. Teach me to rest in the assurance of Your promises rather than in the shifting opinions of others. Let my confidence be rooted in the unfailing love of Christ. In Jesus' name, Amen.

Reflection: Do I live like someone constantly trying to be loved, or someone who already is?

Declaration: If you can be anything, B/YOU.

DAY 33
EQUIPPED FOR EVERY GOOD WORK

Scripture: "…equipped for every good work."—*2 Timothy 3:17 (ESV)*

Devotional Thought: You have everything you need to do what God has called you to do. Stop waiting to feel "ready." If He called you, He's equipped you. Your identity includes divine resources, heavenly backing, and spiritual tools.

Prayer: Lord, I thank You that You have equipped me with everything I need to fulfill my calling. Remind me that I lack nothing when I walk in obedience to You. Strengthen my hands, sharpen my mind, and fill my heart with courage to carry out the works You've prepared for me. Let my service bring glory to Your name and draw others to Your Kingdom. In Jesus' name, Amen.

Reflection: Where do I need to stop second-guessing and start walking in my God-given authority?

Declaration: If you can be anything, B/YOU.

DAY 34

A VESSEL OF HONOR (PART I)

Scripture: "If anyone cleanses himself… he will be a vessel for honor, sanctified and useful for the Master, prepared for every good work." —*2 Timothy 2:21 (NKJV)*

Devotional Thought: You are not disposable—you are a vessel of honor. God has set you apart to carry His glory, not shame. Let Him shape you, fill you, and pour through you. You are useful to the Master—not because you're perfect, but because you're purified.

Prayer: Lord, I thank You that You have called me to be a vessel of honor in Your Kingdom. Purify my heart and remove anything that would keep me from being fully usable for Your glory. Fill me with Your Spirit so that my life carries Your love, power, and truth. May I always be set apart for noble purposes and reflect the holiness of Christ in all that I do. In Jesus' name, Amen.

Reflection: Am I letting God prepare and position me as a vessel for His use?

Declaration: If you can be anything, B/YOU.

DAY 35
CITIZEN OF HEAVEN

Scripture: "But our citizenship is in heaven. And we eagerly await a Savior from there, the Lord Jesus Christ."—*Philippians 3:20 (NIV)*

Devotional Thought: You may live on earth, but your home is in heaven. Your identity is shaped by eternity, not temporary things. Don't get too comfortable here—you are made for more. Represent heaven well and let your life reflect your Kingdom citizenship.

Prayer: Father, thank You that my true citizenship is in heaven. While I walk this earth, anchor my heart in eternity. Help me live aware that I represent Your Kingdom in every space I enter. Detach me from anything temporary that competes with my devotion to You, and align my desires with what lasts forever. Shape my thoughts, words, and actions so they reflect heaven's values—truth, humility, love, and obedience. May my life point others to Christ as I wait with hope and confidence for my Savior. In Jesus' name, Amen.

Reflection: Am I living with eternity in mind or getting distracted by what won't last?

Declaration: If you can be anything, B/YOU.

WEEK 5
PRAYER FOCUS

Father, thank You for the truths revealed this week. Help me to live them out daily, walk in Your strength, and stand firm in my identity in Christ. Let my life bring glory to You. In Jesus' name, Amen.

WEEKLY THOUGHTS

DAY 36
YOU ARE GOD'S TEMPLE

Scripture: "Do you not know that your bodies are temples of the Holy Spirit, who is in you…?"
—*1 Corinthians 6:19 (NIV)*

Devotional Thought: You are not just a shell—you are sacred space. God lives in you. You're not empty or ordinary; you are filled with His Spirit. Treat yourself with the same reverence God does. Protect your peace, guard your gates, and live like the holy vessel you are.

Prayer: Lord, I thank You that my body is the temple of the Holy Spirit. Help me to honor You with my thoughts, words, and actions, keeping my life pure and pleasing in Your sight. Teach me to be sensitive to Your presence that dwells within me. May everything I do reflect the holiness of being Your dwelling place. In Jesus' name, Amen.

Reflection: Am I treating myself like a temple or a trash bin?

Declaration: If you can be anything, B/YOU.

DAY 37

ADOPTED AND ACCEPTED (PART II)

Scripture: "And because we are his children, God has sent the Spirit of his Son into our hearts, prompting us to call out, "Abba, Father." Now you are no longer a slave but God's own child. And since you are his child, God has made you his heir."—*Galatians 4:6-7 (NIV)*

Devotional Thought: Remember, you are not an outsider trying to belong—you're a son or daughter fully accepted. Adoption into God's family means you didn't slip in by accident. He chose you, embraced you, and gave you full access to everything He has.

Prayer: Father, I thank You that I am adopted into Your family through Christ. Help me to rest in the truth that I am accepted by You, no longer an outsider or orphan. Remove every fear of rejection and fill me with confidence in Your love. May I walk daily as Your beloved child, reflecting the security of belonging to You. In Jesus' name, Amen.

Reflection: Do I live like an orphan in the Kingdom or like the child I truly am?

Declaration: If you can be anything, B/YOU.

DAY 38

A ROYAL PRIESTHOOD

Scripture: "...and has made us to be a kingdom and priests to serve his God and Father—to him be glory and power for ever and ever! Amen." —*Revelation 1:6 (NIV)*

Devotional Thought: You are royalty with responsibility. You don't only represent yourself—you represent the King. Your identity isn't just about privilege; it's about purpose. Step into the authority, dignity, and calling that come with being part of God's royal line.

Prayer: Lord, I thank You that You have called me part of a royal priesthood, chosen to declare Your praises. Teach me to carry both the authority of royalty and the humility of a servant. Strengthen me to stand boldly in prayer and intercession for others. Let my life proclaim Your goodness and draw people into Your Kingdom. In Jesus' name, Amen.

Reflection: How would my daily life change if I walked like royalty on assignment?

Declaration: If you can be anything, B/YOU.

DAY 39

MORE THAN A CONQUEROR (PART I)

Scripture: "In all these things we are more than conquerors through Him who loved us." —*Romans 8:37 (NIV)*

Devotional Thought: You're not just scraping by—you're more than a conqueror. God did not build you to break under pressure. The victory you carry goes beyond winning; it transforms. It's the kind of power that turns trials into testimonies.

Prayer: God, I praise You for the victory I already have in Christ. Help me to live with a conqueror's mindset, knowing You have secured the win. Keep me from fear when battles arise and strengthen my faith in You. May my life testify to Your triumph. In Jesus' name, Amen.

Reflection: What battle am I facing that needs a conqueror's mindset?

Declaration: If you can be anything, B/YOU.

DAY 40
ANOINTED FOR IMPACT

Scripture: "Now it is God who makes both us and you stand firm in Christ. He anointed us…" —*2 Corinthians 1:21 (NIV)*

Devotional Thought: You're not just gifted—you're anointed. The anointing sets you apart and empowers you beyond your ability. Your identity includes influence, authority, and divine enablement. When God anoints you, He assigns you—and backs you.

Prayer: Lord, I thank You for the anointing You have placed on my life to make a difference in this world. Remind me that Your Spirit empowers me to impact lives, not for my glory but for Yours. Help me to walk in boldness, using every gift and opportunity to shine Your light. May my influence bring transformation and point others to Christ. In Jesus' name, Amen.

Reflection: Am I walking in my anointing, or am I hiding behind excuses?

Declaration: If you can be anything, B/YOU.

DAY 41
RESTORED

Scripture: "To all who mourn in Israel, he will give a crown of beauty for ashes, a joyous blessing instead of mourning, festive praise instead of despair. In their righteousness, they will be like great oaks that the Lord has planted for his own glory."—*Isaiah 61:3 (NLT)*

Devotional Thought: Your damage does not define you—your redemption defines you. God doesn't just forgive; He restores. He turns shame into stories, mess into miracles, and pain into purpose. Your identity is evidence of His healing power.

Prayer: Lord, thank You for redeeming me and restoring my brokenness. Help me remember that my worth is secured in You, not in my past. Let my story be a testimony of Your grace. Keep me walking in the fullness of Your restoration. In Jesus' name, Amen.

Reflection: What part of my story is God asking me to stop hiding and start sharing?

Declaration: If you can be anything, B/YOU.

DAY 42
CALLED OUT OF DARKNESS

Scripture: "For he has rescued us from the dominion of darkness and brought us into the kingdom of the Son he loves, in whom we have redemption, the forgiveness of sins" —*Colossians 1:13-14 (NIV)*

Devotional Thought: You are called out—on purpose and for purpose. You no longer walk in confusion, shame, or fear. God brought you into light so you can live fully, freely, and faithfully. Your identity is rooted in the fact that you are not who you used to be.

Prayer: Father, I thank You for calling me out of darkness and into Your marvelous light. Remind me daily that I no longer have to live bound by sin or fear. Teach me to walk as a child of light, reflecting Your truth in everything I do. Let my life be a testimony that points others to the freedom found in You. In Jesus' name, Amen.

Reflection: What old identity do I need to leave behind now that I am walking in the light?

Declaration: If you can be anything, B/YOU.

WEEK 6
PRAYER FOCUS

Father, thank You for the truths revealed this week. Help me to live them out daily, walk in Your strength, and stand firm in my identity in Christ. Let my life bring glory to You. In Jesus' name, Amen.

WEEKLY THOUGHTS

DAY 43
FEARFULLY AND WONDERFULLY MADE (PART II)

Scripture: "My frame was not hidden from you when I was made in the secret place, when I was woven together in the depths of the earth."—*Psalm 139:15 (NIV)*

Devotional Thought: God didn't make a mistake when He made you. You're not a rough draft or a second thought—you are intentionally crafted with beauty and purpose. Your identity begins with wonder. Embrace the masterpiece that you are and stop apologizing for your design.

Prayer: Lord, I thank You that I am fearfully and wonderfully made by Your hand. Silence every voice that tells me I am not enough, and replace it with the truth of Your Word. Help me to embrace my uniqueness as a reflection of Your creativity. May I walk confidently, knowing I am a masterpiece of Your design. In Jesus' name, Amen.

Reflection: What part of myself do I need to stop criticizing and start celebrating?

Declaration: If you can be anything, B/YOU.

DAY 44
LIVING LETTERS

Scripture: "You yourselves are our letter, written on our hearts… not with ink but with the Spirit of the living God."—*2 Corinthians 3:2–3 (NIV)*

Devotional Thought: You are a living letter—God's message written through your life. You may never stand on a stage, but your life is preaching. What story is your identity telling? Let people read hope, grace, strength, and truth in the way you live.

Prayer: Father, I thank You that my life is a living letter, written not with ink but by the Spirit of the living God. Help me to live in such a way that others can read Your love and truth through me. Remove anything that distorts or diminishes Your message in my life. Let every word and action reflect Christ clearly to the world around me. In Jesus' name, Amen.

Reflection: What story is my life telling right now?

Declaration: If you can be anything, B/YOU.

DAY 45
COMPLETE IN CHRIST

Scripture: "…you are complete in Him, who is the head of all principality and power." —*Colossians 2:10 (NKJV)*

Devotional Thought: You're not missing anything. In Christ, you lack nothing. Stop waiting on people, titles, or achievements to make you feel "enough." Your identity is whole, not half. What He's placed in you is already complete and functional.

Prayer: Lord, I thank You that in Christ I am whole and lacking nothing. Help me to resist the temptation to seek fulfillment in things or people apart from You. Remind me that my identity, value, and purpose are fully secure in Jesus. Let me live daily from a place of wholeness, resting in the finished work of the cross. In Jesus' name, Amen.

Reflection: Am I looking for completion in things Christ already fulfilled?

Declaration: If you can be anything, B/YOU.

DAY 46
LIGHT OF THE WORLD (PART I)

Scripture: "For you were once darkness, but now you are light in the Lord. Live as children of light (for the fruit of the light consists in all goodness, righteousness and truth)."
—*Ephesians 5:8-9 (NIV)*

Devotional Thought: You are meant for visibility. You are light in dark places. You don't dim to fit in—you shine to stand out. Your identity brings clarity, hope, and truth. You're not meant to be hidden, but to be a city on display for God's glory.

Prayer: Father, thank You for making me the light of the world. Shine through me in every space I enter, even in dark places. Give me courage to stand boldly as a reflection of Your truth. Let my light lead others closer to You. In Jesus' name, Amen.

Reflection: Where have I been dimming my light out of fear or insecurity?

Declaration:If you can be anything, B/YOU.

DAY 47
STEADFAST AND IMMOVABLE

Scripture: "Be steadfast, immovable, always abounding in the work of the Lord..."—*1 Corinthians 15:58 (NKJV)*

Devotional Thought: Your identity isn't swayed by opinions, storms, or seasons. In Christ, you are unshakable. That doesn't mean life won't try to knock you down—but it means you stand anyway. You are built to endure and designed to remain faithful.

Prayer: Lord, I thank You for making me steadfast and immovable in the faith. Strengthen me so that trials, temptations, or distractions will not shake me. Help me to stand firmly on Your Word, rooted and grounded in truth. May my consistency be a testimony of Your power working within me. In Jesus' name, Amen.

Reflection: What has been trying to move me that God has called me to stand through?

Declaration: If you can be anything, B/YOU.

DAY 48
SEATED IN HEAVENLY PLACES

Scripture: "Since, then, you have been raised with Christ, set your hearts on things above, where Christ is, seated at the right hand of God. 2 Set your minds on things above, not on earthly things."—*Colossians 3:1-:2 (NIV)*

Devotional Thought: You're not striving for a seat—you already have one. You are seated in heavenly places with Christ. That means you see things from a higher perspective. Your identity comes with Kingdom authority, eternal access, and divine positioning.

Prayer: Father, I thank You that I am seated with Christ in heavenly places, far above fear, sin, and defeat. Help me to live from this place of victory and not from a posture of striving. Remind me that I have authority in Christ to overcome every scheme of the enemy. Let my perspective always reflect the power of my position in You. In Jesus' name, Amen.

Reflection: Am I living from my heavenly seat or fighting for one on earth?

Declaration: If you can be anything, B/YOU.

DAY 49
SEALED BY THE SPIRIT

Scripture: "When you believed, you were marked in Him with a seal, the promised Holy Spirit…"—*Ephesians 1:13 (NIV)*

Devotional Thought: You are sealed, not shaken. When God sealed you with the Holy Spirit, He stamped you with identity and ownership. The enemy can't steal what's sealed. Let this truth anchor you: You belong to God, and that mark is permanent.

Prayer: Lord, I thank You that I am sealed by the Holy Spirit as a guarantee of my inheritance in You. Remind me that nothing and no one can break the seal of Your promise over my life. Help me to walk in confidence, knowing that I belong to You forever. Let my life display the security and assurance that comes from being marked by Your Spirit. In Jesus' name, Amen.

Reflection: Am I living like someone who's sealed, or someone who still feels unsure?

Declaration: If you can be anything, B/YOU.

WEEK 7
PRAYER FOCUS

Father, thank You for the truths revealed this week. Help me to live them out daily, walk in Your strength, and stand firm in my identity in Christ. Let my life bring glory to You. In Jesus' name, Amen.

WEEKLY THOUGHTS

DAY 50
A TREE PLANTED

Scripture: "They will be like a tree planted by the water that sends out its roots by the stream…"—*Jeremiah 17:8 (NIV)*

Devotional Thought: You are not scattered! You are planted. Your identity is rooted in a Source that never runs dry. Even in drought seasons, you flourish because your nourishment is not from the surface—it's from the Spirit. Be confident in your place. God didn't plant you to fail.

Prayer: Father, I thank You that I am like a tree planted by streams of living water. Keep me rooted in Your Word so that I may stand strong in every season. Let my life bear fruit that blesses others and glorifies You. Guard me from withering in times of trial and help me flourish in Your presence. In Jesus' name, Amen.

Reflection: What area of my life do I need to trust that my roots are stronger than my storms?

Declaration: If you can be anything, B/YOU.

DAY 51

SALT OF THE EARTH (PART II)

Scripture: "Let your conversation be always full of grace, seasoned with salt, so that you may know how to answer everyone."
—*Colossians 4:6 (NIV)*

Devotional Thought: You bring flavor, preservation, and impact. You're not bland or forgettable—your presence makes a difference. Salt changes everything it touches. That's you. Your words, your walk, your witness—it all carries influence. Stay salty in the Spirit.

Prayer: Lord, I thank You for calling me to be salt in the earth, preserving truth and adding the flavor of Your love to every space I enter. Keep me from losing my effectiveness through compromise or fear. Help me to live in such a way that others experience Your grace through me. May my presence draw people closer to You. In Jesus' name, Amen.

Reflection: How am I adding spiritual "flavor" in the spaces I'm called to?

Declaration: If you can be anything, B/YOU.

DAY 52
A BRAND NEW CREATION

Scripture: "I have been crucified with Christ and I no longer live, but Christ lives in me. The life I now live in the body, I live by faith in the Son of God, who loved me and gave himself for me."—*Galatians 2:20 (NIV)*

Devotional Thought: You are not who you used to be. The old you has passed away. Christ reset your identity. That means your past doesn't define you, your mistakes don't own you, and your future is wide open. Embrace the new.

Prayer: Father, thank You that I am a new creation in Christ. Break every chain of my past and remind me of the freedom I have in You. Give me the strength to walk away from shame and step into victory. Let my life be evidence of Your transforming power. In Jesus' name, Amen.

Reflection: What old name or narrative do I need to release today?

Declaration: If you can be anything, B/YOU.

DAY 53
A WORK IN PROGRESS

Scripture: "…He who began a good work in you will carry it on to completion…"—*Philippians 1:6 (NIV)*

Devotional Thought: God doesn't start something He won't finish. You may not be where you want to be yet, but you are becoming. Your identity is not in your perfection—it's in His process. Trust the journey. You're a masterpiece under construction.

Prayer: Father, I thank You that You are faithfully completing the good work You began in me. Help me to be patient with myself as You shape and refine me day by day. Remind me that progress is part of the process and perfection is found only in You. Let my life continually reflect Your transforming grace. In Jesus' name, Amen.

Reflection: How can I give myself permission to grow without guilt?

Declaration: If you can be anything, B/YOU.

DAY 54
SET APART (PART I)

Scripture: "But just as he who called you is holy, so be holy in all you do; for it is written: "Be holy, because I am holy.""—*1 Peter 1:15-16 (NIV)*

Devotional Thought: You were different before you were born. Set apart doesn't mean strange—it means sacred. You weren't made to blend in but to stand out for a divine reason. God marked you for something holy. Walk like you're chosen.

Prayer: Lord, I thank You that You have set me apart for Your glory and purposes. Guard my heart from the temptation to blend in with the world when You've called me to stand out. Fill me with courage to walk in holiness and obedience to Your Word. Let my life shine as evidence that I belong fully to You. In Jesus' name, Amen.

Reflection: Where am I tempted to conform rather than embrace my calling?

Declaration: If you can be anything, B/YOU.

DAY 55

A FRIEND OF GOD (PART II)

Scripture: "The Lord confides in those who fear him; he makes his covenant known to them." —*Psalm 25:14 (NIV)*

Devotional Thought: God isn't distant—He's relational. You are His friend, not just His follower. That's identity rooted in intimacy. You can talk to Him, walk with Him, and trust that He shares His heart with you. Friendship with God is a high honor.

Prayer: Father, I thank You for the privilege of being called Your friend. Draw me closer to You so that I may know Your heart and walk in step with Your will. Remove distractions that try to steal my attention and deepen my intimacy with You. Let my life reflect the joy and honor of true friendship with the living God. In Jesus' name, Amen.

Reflection: Am I keeping God at a distance when He wants closeness?

Declaration: If you can be anything, B/YOU.

DAY 56
HIS WORKMANSHIP

Scripture: "But now, O LORD, thou art our father; we are the clay, and thou our potter; and we all are the work of thy hand."—*Isaiah 64:8 (KJV)*

Devotional Thought: You are God's craftsmanship—His custom design. Not mass produced, not duplicated. He wrote your story line by line, with purpose, grace, and glory. When you understand that, comparison dies. You can't copy what was created to stand alone.

Prayer: God, thank You for forming me with intention and care. Help me embrace who You created me to be without comparison or doubt. Let me walk confidently as Your workmanship, fully secure in Your purpose for my life. In Jesus' name, Amen.

Reflection: Where have I been undervaluing God's unique creation—me?

Declaration: If you can be anything, B/YOU.

WEEK 8
PRAYER FOCUS

Father, thank You for the truths revealed this week. Help me to live them out daily, walk in Your strength, and stand firm in my identity in Christ. Let my life bring glory to You. In Jesus' name, Amen.

WEEKLY THOUGHTS

DAY 57
THE APPLE OF HIS EYE

Scripture: "Keep me as the apple of Your eye; hide me under the shadow of Your wings." —*Psalm 17:8 (NKJV)*

Devotional Thought: You are treasured and watched over. Being the "apple of His eye" means you are constantly on God's mind and deeply loved. He guards you, values you, and delights in you. You are not overlooked—you are the focus of His affection.

Prayer: Father, I thank You that I am the apple of Your eye, cherished and deeply loved by You. Remind me that I am never overlooked or forgotten in Your sight. Guard me with the same care and tenderness that Your Word promises. Let my confidence grow from knowing I am precious in Your presence. In Jesus' name, Amen.

Reflection: Do I see myself the way God sees me—worthy of love and protection?

Declaration: If you can be anything, B/YOU.

DAY 58
GOD'S AMBASSADOR

Scripture: "We are therefore Christ's ambassadors, as though God were making His appeal through us."—*2 Corinthians 5:20 (NIV)*

Devotional Thought: You don't just live here—you represent heaven. As an ambassador, your identity is tied to your mission. You speak for the Kingdom. You live as a reflection of the One who sent you. You carry peace, truth, and purpose into every place you step.

Prayer: Lord, I thank You that You have called me to be an ambassador for Christ, representing Your Kingdom here on earth. Help me to speak with wisdom, act with integrity, and carry myself with humility so others may see You through me. Remind me that I am not my own, but a messenger of Your love and reconciliation. Let my life reflect heaven's culture wherever I go. In Jesus' name, Amen.

Reflection: How does being God's representative shape the way I carry myself?

Declaration: If you can be anything, B/YOU.

DAY 59
COVERED BY GRACE

Scripture: "My grace is sufficient for you, for My power is made perfect in weakness." —*2 Corinthians 12:9 (NIV)*

Devotional Thought: Your weakness doesn't limit your identity—your identity is covered by grace. You don't have to be flawless to be favored. God's grace makes up the difference, and His strength shines where yours fades. You are enough because His grace is on you.

Prayer: Father, I thank You that Your grace covers every weakness, failure, and shortcoming in my life. Teach me to rest in the sufficiency of Your grace instead of striving in my own strength. When I fall, remind me that Your mercy lifts me and sets me back on course. Let my life be a testimony of the power of grace that sustains and transforms me daily. In Jesus' name, Amen.

Reflection: Where do I need to stop striving and let grace take the lead?

Declaration: If you can be anything, B/YOU.

DAY 60

A VESSEL OF HONOR (PART II)

Scripture: "…and that He might make known the riches of His glory on the vessels of mercy, which He had prepared beforehand for glory…"—*Romans 9:23 (NKJV)*

Devotional Thought: Remember, you are not disposable—you are durable. A vessel of honor is purified, set apart, and ready for purpose. You carry glory. You're not just carrying potential—you're carrying promise. God doesn't waste what He's refined.

Prayer: Lord, I thank You that You have called me to be a vessel of honor, useful for Your Kingdom and prepared for every good work. Purify my heart and cleanse me from anything that would make me unfit for Your purpose. Fill me with Your Spirit so that my life overflows with Your love and truth. May I always reflect the holiness and integrity of being set apart for You. In Jesus' name, Amen.

Reflection: Do I see myself as valuable or as someone God tolerates?

Declaration: If you can be anything, B/YOU.

DAY 61

EMPOWERED BY THE SPIRIT (PART II)

Scripture: "So he said to me, 'This is the word of the Lord to Zerubbabel: Not by might nor by power, but by my Spirit,' says the Lord Almighty."—*Zechariah 4:6 (NIV)*

Devotional Thought: The Spirit equips you for every task, gives wisdom beyond your years, and grants courage when fear tries to rise. You are Spirit-empowered to walk boldly in your calling.

Prayer: Holy Spirit, I thank You for empowering me with Your strength, wisdom, and presence. Remind me that I can do nothing in my own ability, but all things through Your power. Stir up the gifts within me and give me boldness to use them for Your glory. Let my life be a demonstration of Your Spirit working in and through me. In Jesus' name, Amen.

Reflection: What area of my life needs to tap into the power of God's Spirit?

Declaration: If you can be anything, B/YOU.

DAY 62
FREE INDEED
(PART II)

Scripture: "Now the Lord is the Spirit, and where the Spirit of the Lord is, there is freedom."—*2 Corinthians 3:17 (NIV)*

Devotional Thought: You don't have a taste of freedom—you have full access. Free from shame. Free from sin. Free from people's opinions. Your identity is rooted in liberty, not bondage. You are free indeed—and you don't have to go back.

Prayer: Jesus, I celebrate the freedom You gave

me through the cross. Help me never to return to the things that once held me captive. Teach me to live with joy as one who has been set free. May my freedom point others back to You. In Jesus' name, Amen.

Reflection: What old chains am I tempted to pick up again?

Declaration: If you can be anything, B/YOU.

DAY 63
CALLED BY NAME

Scripture: "I have called you by name; you are Mine."—*Isaiah 43:1 (NIV)*

Devotional Thought: God didn't just call you—He called you by name. That means He knows every detail and still says, "You're Mine." You're not just one in the crowd. Your identity is personal to Him. He called you specifically, intentionally, and lovingly.

Prayer: Father, I thank You that You know me by name and have called me into a relationship with You. Remind me that I am not forgotten or overlooked, but I chose with intention and love.

Help me to walk in confidence, knowing that Your call on my life carries purpose and destiny. Let my response to Your voice always be "yes." In Jesus' name, Amen.

Reflection: Have I been answering to names that God never gave me?

Declaration: If you can be anything, B/YOU.

WEEK 9
PRAYER FOCUS

Father, thank You for the truths revealed this week. Help me to live them out daily, walk in Your strength, and stand firm in my identity in Christ. Let my life bring glory to You. In Jesus' name, Amen.

WEEKLY THOUGHTS

DAY 64

MORE THAN A CONQUEROR (PART II)

Scripture: "You, dear children, are from God and have overcome them, because the one who is in you is greater than the one who is in the world."—*1 John 4:4 (NIV)*

Devotional Thought: You are an overcomer. In Christ, you don't just win; you win with purpose, power, and peace. Your identity isn't tied to defeat. You are more than what you've been through—you are a conqueror with a testimony.

Prayer: God, I praise You for the victory I already have in Christ. Help me to live with a conqueror's mindset, knowing You have secured the win. Keep me from fear when battles arise and strengthen my faith in You. May my life testify to Your triumph. In Jesus' name, Amen.

Reflection: What battles has Christ conquered for me?

Declaration: If you can be anything, B/YOU.

DAY 65
CROWNED WITH GLORY

Scripture: "You made them a little lower than the angels and crowned them with glory and honor."—*Psalm 8:5 (NIV)*

Devotional Thought: You don't need to chase crowns—the Lord already crowned you. Honor is part of your identity. The world may not recognize it, but heaven does. Don't let people's opinions strip you of what God has placed on your head. Walk like royalty.

Prayer: Lord, I thank You that You have crowned me with glory and honor as Your child. Remind me that my worth is not defined by the world but by Your blessing and favor upon my life. Teach me to walk humbly, carrying this crown with gratitude and reverence. Let my life reflect the dignity of being chosen and honored by You. In Jesus' name, Amen.

Reflection: Am I living like someone crowned with glory or someone desperate for it?

Declaration: If you can be anything, B/YOU.

DAY 66
THE TEMPLE OF THE HOLY SPIRIT

Scripture: "Don't you know that you yourselves are God's temple and that God's Spirit dwells in your midst?"—*1 Corinthians 3:16 (NIV)*

Devotional Thought: Your identity isn't just spiritual—it's sacred. You are the living, breathing home of God's Spirit. That makes you holy ground. What you allow in and around you matters. Honor yourself because you house His presence.

Prayer: Father, Thank you for making me your

dwelling place. Help me to honor my body, my choices and my life as a temple of the Holy Spirit. Teach me to walk with awareness and reverence for Your presence within me. In Jesus' name, Amen.

Reflection: Am I treating my body and life like a dwelling place for God?

Declaration: If you can be anything, B/YOU.

DAY 67
THE WORK OF HIS HANDS

Scripture: "The works of the Lord are great…His work is honorable and glorious…"—*Psalm 111: 2–3 (KJV)*

Devotional Thought: You are His handiwork, not happenstance. God doesn't create chaos—He establishes beauty, function, and brilliance. Your identity is proof of His excellence. When you doubt your worth, remember whose hands formed you.

Prayer: Lord, I thank You that I am the work of Your hands, carefully crafted with intention and love. Remind me that I am not a mistake but a masterpiece shaped by Your wisdom. Teach me to value myself as You do and to use my life for the purpose You designed. Let my words and actions display the beauty of being created by You. In Jesus' name, Amen.

Reflection: How does knowing I am handcrafted by God change how I view myself?

Declaration: If you can be anything, B/YOU.

DAY 68
DELIVERED FOR DESTINY

Scripture: "He brought them out… that He might bring them in…"—*Deuteronomy 6:23 (KJV)*

Devotional Thought: God brought you out of darkness for a reason. Deliverance was never the end goal—destiny is. God didn't free you for you to sit still. He rescued you to release you into purpose. Your identity includes movement and mission.

Prayer: Father, I thank You for delivering me from bondage and setting me free to walk in my destiny. Remind me that every chain broken was not just for my freedom but to position me for purpose. Help me to live with courage, knowing my past no longer defines me. Let my life testify to Your power to redeem and direct my steps. In Jesus' name, Amen.

Reflection: Am I living like someone rescued for a reason?

Declaration: If you can be anything, B/YOU.

DAY 69
GOD'S MASTER PLAN

Scripture: "For I know the plans I have for you… plans to give you a hope and a future." —*Jeremiah 29:11 (NIV)*

Devotional Thought: You are not random. You are part of a master plan. Even in detours, delays, and disappointments, your identity remains tied to divine design. God's plan is still intact, and His intentions for you are still good.

Prayer: Father, I'm excited about the plans You have for my life—plans filled with hope and purpose. Help me trust Your design, even when the path is unclear, and walk forward with confidence in Your goodness. In Jesus' name, Amen.

Reflection: Have I trusted God's plan for others more than I've trusted His plan for me?

Declaration: If you can be anything, B/YOU.

DAY 70
PART OF THE BODY

Scripture: "Now you are the body of Christ, and each one of you is a part of it."—*1 Corinthians 12:27 (NIV)*

Devotional Thought: You belong. Your identity includes community. You're not just a believer—you're a body part. You're needed. You're useful. You're valuable. Don't downplay your position or isolate yourself. You fit because He placed you.

Prayer: Lord, I thank You that I am part of the body of Christ, joined with brothers and sisters in Your family. Teach me to value unity, honor diversity, and serve with love. Remind me that each member has a purpose, and together we reflect Your fullness. Let my role build up the body and glorify You. In Jesus' name, Amen.

Reflection: What would change if I believed the body of Christ needs me?

Declaration: If you can be anything, B/YOU.

WEEK 10
PRAYER FOCUS

Father, thank You for the truths revealed this week. Help me to live them out daily, walk in Your strength, and stand firm in my identity in Christ. Let my life bring glory to You. In Jesus' name, Amen.

WEEKLY THOUGHTS

DAY 71
SEATED WITH CHRIST (PART II)

Scripture: "Let us then approach God's throne of grace with confidence, so that we may receive mercy and find grace to help us in our time of need."—*Hebrews 4:16 (NIV)*

Devotional Thought: You're not fighting for victory—you're operating from it. Your position in Christ is one of authority, not anxiety. You are seated in a place of rest, power, and access. You're above the chaos because you're seated with the King.

Prayer: Father, I thank You that I am seated with Christ in heavenly places, lifted above every power and distraction of this world. Remind me to live from a place of victory and not defeat. Help me to see my life through the lens of eternity and to walk in the authority You've given me. Let my confidence always come from knowing I share this seat with Jesus. In His name, Amen.

Reflection: Am I standing in my authority or settling in insecurity?

Declaration: If you can be anything, B/YOU.

DAY 72
LIGHT OF THE WORLD (PART II)

Scripture: "...so that you may become blameless and pure, "children of God without fault in a warped and crooked generation." Then you will shine among them like stars in the sky"—*Philippians 2:15 (NIV)*

Devotional Thought: Light is your identity—bright, radiant, and unavoidable. When the world gets darker, your purpose gets clearer. You carry the brilliance of heaven to reveal truth and love in every dark place.

Prayer: Father, thank You for making me the light of the world. Shine through me in every space I enter, even in dark places. Give me the courage to stand boldly as a reflection of Your truth. Let my light lead others closer to You. In Jesus' name, Amen.

Reflection: Where is God calling me to shine unapologetically?

Declaration: If you can be anything, B/YOU.

DAY 73
CHOSEN GENERATION

Scripture: "You *are* My witnesses," says the Lord, and My servant whom I have chosen, that you may know and believe Me, and understand that I *am* He. Before Me there was no God formed, nor shall there be after Me."—*Isaiah 43:10 (NKJV)*

Devotional Thought: You didn't miss your moment—you are here on purpose. God selected you for now. You're part of a generation anointed to break cycles, shift culture, and carry glory. You are chosen, not just to belong, but to build.

Prayer: Lord, thank You for choosing me before anyone else ever knew my name. Help me to live boldly as someone handpicked by You. Let me not chase after the approval of others but rest in the truth that I belong to You. Remind me each day that I am set apart for divine purpose. In Jesus' name, Amen.

Reflection: What does it look like for me to live chosen in my generation?

Declaration: If you can be anything, B/YOU.

DAY 74
FEARFULLY AND WONDERFULLY MADE (PART III)

Scripture: "Your eyes saw my unformed body; all the days ordained for me were written in your book before one of them came to be."—*Psalm 139:16 (NIV)*

Devotional Thought: You are not flawed—you are fascinating. God made you with wonder and intention. You don't need to shrink, fix, or compare. Every part of you has purpose woven in. Your identity is not a mistake—it's a miracle.

Prayer: Lord, I thank You that I am fearfully and wonderfully made, crafted with precision and love by Your hands. Remind me that my worth is not measured by the world but by Your design. Silence every lie that tells me I am less than who You created me to be. Help me to embrace my uniqueness and walk boldly in the identity You gave me. In Jesus' name, Amen.

Reflection: Am I praising God for the way He made me—or apologizing for it?

Declaration: If you can be anything, B/YOU.

DAY 75
NO LONGER A SLAVE

Scripture: "So you are no longer a slave, but God's child; and since you are His child, God has made you also an heir."—*Galatians 4:7 (NIV)*

Devotional Thought: You're not bound—you're bloodline. You don't live like a servant trying to earn love. You are a child of the King with full access to His promises. Break free from any mindset that says you don't belong. You're not on the outside—you're in the family.

Prayer: Father, I thank You that I am no longer a slave to sin, fear, or shame, but free through Christ Jesus. Remind me daily that I am adopted into Your family, and I belong to You. Help me to walk in the boldness of freedom, leaving behind every chain of the past. Let my life declare the liberty I have in You. In Jesus' name, Amen.

Reflection: What am I still serving that I am already free from?

Declaration: If you can be anything, B/YOU.

DAY 76
HIS MASTERPIECE

Scripture: "See, I have written your name on the palms of my hands. Always in my mind is a picture of Jerusalem's walls in ruins." —*Isaiah 49:16 (NLT)*

Devotional Thought: A masterpiece isn't rushed, replicated, or revised—it's revered. That's what God calls you. His finest work. You're not basic, broken, or boring. You're an original design meant to reflect His creativity, love, and glory.

Prayer: Father, thank You for forming me with intention and calling me Your masterpiece.

When my flaws try to speak louder than Your truth, quiet every lie and anchor my heart in who You say I am. Teach me to rest in Your work, trust Your process, and walk fully aligned with the purpose You placed within me. In Jesus' name, Amen.

Reflection: Do I see myself as a masterpiece or just a mess?

Declaration: If you can be anything, B/YOU.

DAY 77
AUTHORED BY GOD

Scripture: "Looking unto Jesus, the author and finisher of our faith…"—*Hebrews 12:2 (KJV)*

Devotional Thought: God didn't just start your story—He's writing every word. And he never leaves a story unfinished. Your identity is not in your past chapter but in the Author's pen. Trust the plot twists. The end will be glorious because He wrote it.

Prayer: Lord, I thank You that my story is authored by Your hand and not by chance. Remind me that every chapter of my life has purpose, even the ones I don't fully understand. Help me to trust the process, knowing You are writing something beautiful for Your glory. Let my life reflect the masterpiece of Your authorship. In Jesus' name, Amen.

Reflection: Where am I tempted to take the pen from God's hand?

Declaration: If you can be anything, B/YOU.

WEEK 11
PRAYER FOCUS

Father, thank You for the truths revealed this week. Help me to live them out daily, walk in Your strength, and stand firm in my identity in Christ. Let my life bring glory to You. In Jesus' name, Amen.

WEEKLY THOUGHTS

DAY 78
GUARDED BY PEACE

Scripture: "And the peace of God, which surpasses all understanding, will guard your hearts and your minds in Christ Jesus." —*Philippians 4:7 (ESV)*

Devotional Thought: Your identity comes with divine protection. Peace isn't just a feeling—it's a guard. It keeps your mind from wandering and your heart from breaking under pressure. You don't need to lose yourself to stay calm. Peace is your portion.

Prayer: Father, I thank You for the peace of God that guards my heart and mind in Christ Jesus.

When anxiety or fear tries to rise, remind me that Your peace is stronger than every storm. Help me to rest in the calm assurance that You are in control. Let Your peace overflow in me so others may encounter Your presence through my life. In Jesus' name, Amen.

Reflection: Where do I need to stop fighting and start letting peace guard me?

Declaration: If you can be anything, B/YOU.

DAY 79
COMPLETE IN HIM

Scripture: "And you are complete in Him, who is the head of all principality and power." —*Colossians 2:10 (NKJV)*

Devotional Thought: Nothing is missing in you that God hasn't already filled. You don't need the approval of people or the applause of the crowd. In Christ, you are complete—not lacking, not leftover, not less than. You are whole.

Prayer: Lord, I thank You that in Christ I am whole, complete, and lacking nothing. Silence the lies that tell me I am unfinished or unworthy. Teach me to rest in the fullness of who You are instead of striving in my own strength. Let my life reflect the wholeness that comes only from being complete in You. In Jesus' name, Amen.

Reflection: What am I trying to add to my identity that God already completed?

Declaration: If you can be anything, B/YOU.

DAY 80
SALT OF THE EARTH (PART III)

Scripture: "For we are to God the pleasing aroma of Christ among those who are being saved and those who are perishing." —*2 Corinthians 2:15 (NIV)*

Devotional Thought: Salt preserves, flavors, and heals. So do you. Your presence should enhance environments and preserve truth. You are not bland—you're bold. Your identity isn't just in what you say, but in how you season the world around you.

Prayer: Father, I thank You for making me the salt of the earth, chosen to bring flavor and preservation to the world around me. Keep my influence strong and pure, never diluted by compromise. Help me to live in such a way that my words and actions stir a hunger for You in others. Let my life point people toward the hope and truth found in Christ. In Jesus' name, Amen.

Reflection: Am I blending in, or am I bringing the flavor of Christ?

Declaration: If you can be anything, B/YOU.

DAY 81
IN THE BELOVED

Scripture: "…He made us accepted in the Beloved."—*Ephesians 1:6 (NKJV)*

Devotional Thought: You don't have to beg for belonging. In Christ, you are already accepted—already loved. You are not tolerated, you are treasured. Stop trying to earn what God has already extended. You are His beloved.

Prayer: Lord, I thank You that I am accepted in the Beloved and fully embraced by your love. Remind me that my worth is not in what I do but in who I am in Christ. Help me live daily in the security of your acceptance and not in the opinions of others. Let my life reflect the joy and freedom of being loved by You. In Jesus' name, Amen.

Reflection: Where am I still seeking acceptance from people more than God?

Declaration: If you can be anything, B/YOU.

DAY 82
ROOTED AND BUILT UP

Scripture: "...that Christ may dwell in your hearts through faith; that you, being rooted and grounded in love, may be able to comprehend with all the saints what *is* the width and length and depth and height, to know the love of Christ which passes knowledge; that you may be filled with all the fullness of God."—*Ephesians 3:17 (NKJV)*

Devotional Thought: Your identity is not shallow—it's secure. You're not called to grow tall. You are called to grow deep. When your roots are in Christ, no storm can shake your foundation. Your strength is in how deeply you know who you are in Him.

Prayer: Father, I thank You that my life is rooted in Christ and built up by Your Word. Strengthen my foundation so that I remain unshaken when storms arise. Help me grow deeper in my faith and stronger in my character each day. Let my roots draw from Your love so that I flourish and bear fruit for Your glory. In Jesus' name, Amen.

Reflection: Am I focusing more on surface-level growth or deep spiritual roots?

Declaration: If you can be anything, B/YOU.

DAY 83
SET APART (PART II)

Scripture: "Do not conform to the pattern of this world, but be transformed by the renewing of your mind. Then you will be able to test and approve what God's will is—his good, pleasing and perfect will."—*Romans 12:2 (NIV)*

Devotional Thought: You weren't born to blend in. You were set apart to stand out. God didn't call you to copy others—He called you to reflect Him. Your difference is your destiny. Embrace your uniqueness. There's power in your purpose.

Prayer: Lord, I thank You that You have set me apart to live for You. Keep me from blending into the patterns of the world and strengthen me to walk in holiness. Remind me that being set apart is a privilege that positions me to reflect Your glory. Let my life be a living testimony of Your love and power at work in me. In Jesus' name, Amen.

Reflection: Where have I been trying to fit in when God has set me apart?

Declaration: If you can be anything, B/YOU.

DAY 84
LIVING EPISTLE

Scripture: "Let your light so shine before men, that they may see your good works and glorify your Father in heaven."—*Matthew 5:16 (NKJV)*

Devotional Thought: You're more than a person—you're a message. Your life speaks of grace, redemption, and glory. People may never read a Bible, but they'll read you. Let your identity in Christ be clear, consistent, and contagious.

Prayer: Father, I thank You that my life is a living epistle, written by Your Spirit for others to read. Help me to live with integrity so that my actions align with Your Word. Remove anything that clouds or distorts the message of Christ in me. Let every chapter of my life reflect Your love and draw others closer to You. In Jesus' name, Amen.

Reflection: What is my life saying to those who are watching?

Declaration: If you can be anything, B/YOU.

WEEK 12
PRAYER FOCUS

Father, thank You for the truths revealed this week. Help me to live them out daily, walk in Your strength, and stand firm in my identity in Christ. Let my life bring glory to You. In Jesus' name, Amen.

WEEKLY THOUGHTS

DAY 85
DESIGNED ON PURPOSE

Scripture: "...for it is God who works in you both to will and to do for *His* good pleasure."—*Philippians 2:13 (NKJV)*

Devotional Thought: You are not a random project—you are a masterpiece in progress. God shaped you intentionally and designed you for good. You were born with a purpose already assigned, not something you have to invent. Walk confidently knowing you are made on purpose, for purpose.

Prayer: Father, thank You for creating me with intention and assigning purpose to my life before I ever began. You do all things well. Help me walk confidently in the good works You prepared for me, trusting Your design and Your timing. In Jesus' name, Amen.

Reflection: What "good work" is God calling me to walk in today?

Declaration: If you can be anything, B/YOU.

DAY 86

CALLED ACCORDING TO HIS PURPOSE

Scripture: "And we know that all things work together for good…to those who are called according to His purpose."—*Romans 8:28 (NKJV)*

Devotional Thought: Your identity is connected to a divine purpose, and it cannot be derailed. Even your detours are directed. What the enemy meant to disqualify you, God is using to equip you. You're not just called—you're covered.

Prayer: Lord, I thank You that I am called according to Your purpose and not by accident. Remind me that every season of my life is working together for good because I love You. Give me the courage to walk boldly in the assignment you've given me. Let my life fulfill the purpose for which I was created and bring glory to Your name. In Jesus' name, Amen.

Reflection: Where has God turned my pain into purpose?

Declaration: If you can be anything, B/YOU.

DAY 87
THE VINE AND THE BRANCHES

Scripture: "I am the vine; you are the branches. If you remain in Me and I in you, you will bear much fruit…"—*John 15:5 (NIV)*

Devotional Thought: Your identity doesn't grow from effort—it grows from connection. Staying connected to Christ produces fruit without forcing it. You don't have to strive, just stay. The fruit is the proof of where you're rooted.

Prayer: Father, I thank You that Jesus is the vine, and I am a branch connected to Him. Keep me abiding in Your presence so that my life bears lasting fruit. Protect me from trying to live in my own strength, apart from You. Let everything I produce flow from intimacy with Christ and bring glory to Your name. In Jesus' name, Amen.

Reflection: Am I working hard to impress God, or am I staying close enough to reflect Him?

Declaration: If you can be anything, B/YOU.

DAY 88

FILLED WITH THE SPIRIT

Scripture: "Do not get drunk on wine… Instead, be filled with the Spirit."—*Ephesians 5:18 (NIV)*

Devotional Thought: Being filled isn't a one-time experience—it's a lifestyle. The Holy Spirit empowers, comforts, and reminds you who you really are. When you're full of Him, you don't have to chase validation. You walk in clarity, boldness, and identity.

Prayer: Lord, I thank You for filling me with the Holy Spirit, who guides, strengthens, and empowers me. Teach me to yield daily to the Holy Spirit's leading and not to lean on my own understanding. Let your presence influence my words, actions, and thoughts. May my life overflow with the fruit of the Holy Spirit and draw others closer to You. In Jesus' name, Amen.

Reflection: What fills me that competes with the Holy Spirit?

Declaration: If you can be anything, B/YOU.

DAY 89
TRANSFORMED BY THE RENEWING

Scripture: "Be transformed by the renewing of your mind…"—*Romans 12:2 (NIV)*

Devotional Thought: Who you believe you are will shape how you live. Transformation doesn't begin in your actions—it begins in your thoughts. God is after your mind because when your thinking shifts, your identity aligns. You are not who the world says you are. You are who God says you are.

Prayer: Father, I thank You that transformation comes through the renewing of my mind by Your Word. Cleanse my thoughts from lies, fear, and doubt, and replace them with truth, faith, and hope. Teach me to think in alignment with Heaven so that my life reflects Christ more each day. Let my mind be a testimony of the power of Your Spirit to change me from the inside out. In Jesus' name, Amen.

Reflection: What thoughts about myself do I need to surrender to God?

Declaration: If you can be anything, B/YOU.

DAY 90
HIDDEN WITH CHRIST IN GOD

Scripture: "For you died, and your life is now hidden with Christ in God."—*Colossians 3:3 (NIV)*

Devotional Thought: Your true self is not exposed to the world—it's hidden in Christ. That means your value is safe, your identity is protected, and your purpose is secure. When the world tries to redefine you, remember: your identity is wrapped in Him.

Prayer: Lord, I thank You that my life is hidden with Christ in God, safe and secure in Your love.

Teach me to rest in the covering of Your presence instead of striving for the approval of others. Protect me from the distractions of the world and keep my heart anchored in eternity. Let my hidden life in You produce fruit that glorifies Christ. In Jesus' name, Amen.

Reflection: Am I hiding my identity from people or hiding it in Christ?

Declaration: If you can be anything, B/YOU.

AUTHOR'S NOTE

Congratulations!

You have completed the 90-day journey of discovering and living your identity in Christ. Concluding this book is not the end—it's the launch. Continue to live authentically, purposefully, and powerfully in who God created you to be.

MEET TIA COOPER

Tia Cooper is a prophetic voice called to host, steward, and release the Presence of the Lord. With a mantle for intercession, identity, and transformation, she ministers with boldness, purity, and uncompromising obedience to the will of God. Her life and ministry echo the cry of Exodus 33:15, "If Your Presence does not go with us, do not send us from here."

She holds a Bachelor of Science in Psychology from North Carolina Agricultural and Technical State University, a foundation that uniquely supports her calling to minister healing, identity, and purpose to God's people.

Tia is the visionary and founder of B/YOU, a prophetic movement divinely conceived during an encounter with God while driving down I-485. In that moment, the Lord spoke clearly to her heart, revealing the power of authenticity and identity in

Him. B/YOU is a heaven-inspired mandate calling believers to shed fear, comparison, and performance, and to walk fully in who God created them to be. As declared in Psalm 139:14, "I praise You because I am fearfully and wonderfully made."

Tia has been instrumental in helping believers discover, embrace, and walk in their identity in Christ, activating them to live free from labels, past wounds, and limitations. Her ministry reflects 2 Corinthians 5:17, "If anyone is in Christ, he is a new creation."

Based in Charlotte, North Carolina, Tia is a devoted mother to her son, Tyler Hill. While intercession and communion with God remain her greatest passion, she also treasures time with family and friends.

Her life's message and prophetic declaration remain clear:

"If you can be anything… B/YOU."

For when you become who God created you to be, you glorify Him fully (Matthew 5:16).
Connect with Tia on the web:
- **Facebook:** @tia.cooper.94
- **Instagram:** @iamtiacooper
- **Website:** https://www.tiacooper.org/